PRESENTED TO:

_____

"*The* LORD *will open the heavens, the storehouse of his bounty, to send rain on your land in season and to bless all the work of your hands.*"

DEUTERONOMY 28:12

PRESENTED BY:

_____

DATE:

_____

BLESSED
BY GOD

Harrison House
Tulsa, Oklahoma

Declarations for Your Life written by James Riddle.

Compilation, writing, and composition of devotions by Christy Phillippe in association with Bordon Books, Tulsa, Oklahoma.

10 09 08 07 06   10 9 8 7 6 5 4 3 2 1

Blessed by God
ISBN 1-57794-804-1
Copyright © 2006 by Harrison House, Inc.

Published by **Harrison House, Inc.**
P.O. Box 35035
Tulsa, Oklahoma 74153

INTRODUCTION

Let God's blessings overtake you! Living in the busy world of today can keep you distracted from realizing the many blessings that God has promised you. When you take a few moments to reflect on the good things you have, your outlook on life changes. Your hopes rise and your faith in God's promises brings even more blessings to your life.

Let this book refresh you and remind you that God loves you and always has your best interest at heart. Be thankful and rejoice that you truly are *blessed by God.*

ot long before his death, Henri Nouwen wrote about some friends of his, called the Flying Roudellas, who were trapeze artists.

They told Henri that there is a special relationship between flyer and catcher on the trapeze. The flyer is the one who lets go, and the catcher is the one who catches. As the flyer swings high above the crowd on the trapeze, the moment comes when he must let go. He arcs out into the air. His job is to remain as still as possible and wait for the strong hands of the catcher to pluck him from the air.

One of the Flying Roudellas told Henri, "The flyer must never try to catch the catcher." The flyer must wait in absolute trust. The catcher will catch him, but he must wait.

What a blessing it is to wait on the Lord! He is trustworthy—He will always catch us when we place our faith in Him.

He giveth power to the faint; and to them
that have no might he increaseth strength.
Even the youths shall faint and be weary,
and the young men shall utterly fall: But they
that wait upon the Lord shall renew their
strength; they shall mount up with wings
as eagles; they shall run, and not be weary;
and they shall walk, and not faint.

ISAIAH 40:29–31 KJV

DECLARATION FOR YOUR LIFE

*The Lord is my strength and my life. He is faithful to
me and increases my power so that I can be confident
in every situation. Even youths get tired and young
men stumble and fall, but I have my hope in the Lord.
He renews my strength and spiritual force, making me
soar on wings like an eagle. I run my race and never
burn out. So long as I stay focused on Him, I will
never grow weary in my walk with Jesus.*

here is a fierce storm that has come up on the tiny boat in the middle of the Sea of Galilee. The disciples of Jesus are terror stricken. The storm threatens to overwhelm them. As the water begins to fill the boat, they work feverishly to keep it from sinking. Where is Jesus while this is happening? Incredibly, there He lay, fast asleep, in the boat. The disciples awaken Him. "Lord," they say, "don't You care that we are perishing?" Jesus, now fully awake, speaks three words to the raging storm: "Peace, be still!" In a moment's notice, the winds die down, the waves subside, and a supernatural calm settles over the awestruck company of disciples.

Now, fast-forward to the raging circumstances in your own life. Hear the words of Jesus speak to your heart: *My child, I am here. It will be okay. Turn it over to Me. Trust Me. Peace, be still.*

Peace I leave with you, my peace I give
unto you: not as the world giveth,
give I unto you. Let not your heart
be troubled, neither let it be afraid.

JOHN 14:27 KJV

DECLARATION FOR YOUR LIFE

I have at this moment the very peace of Jesus within my heart. It is mine forever. He will never take it from me. I will not allow my heart to be troubled or afraid. In Jesus, I have a boldness of faith and confidence that puts me over in every situation.

ight-year-old Jonathan, an avid hockey player, entered a contest to see a Colorado Avalanche National Hockey League game—and he lost. Despite his tears of disappointment, his mom said, "If the desire of your heart is to go to an Avalanche game, you should pray about it." So Jonathan did.

Jonathan's dad didn't know about his prayer, but that night he came home from work and announced that a friend had given him tickets to watch the Avalanche practice. While there, they sat just in front of the glass surrounding the ice. Thrilled to be so close, Jonathan watched his favorite player, Patrick Roy, at work.

Suddenly, Patrick Roy skated over to the bench. He had broken the blade on his hockey stick. As the trainer handed him a new stick, Roy looked at Jonathan and pointed. The trainer took the broken stick and handed it over the glass to the boy.

Patrick Roy's stick now hangs on Jonathan's wall, but it is more than just a precious souvenir. It reminds him of God's goodness. God always has our best and His glory in mind, and He is able to answer our prayers with more than we could ask or imagine.

May the Lord, the God of your fathers, make you a thousand times as many as you are and bless you as He has promised you!

DEUTERONOMY 1:11 AMP

DECLARATION FOR YOUR LIFE

My heavenly Father, the God of my forefathers, increases me and blesses me with His abundance just as He has promised. I lack no good thing. My walk in this earth is as if I am walking through a great wilderness. The world system is so contrary to my new nature that I am like a stranger in a strange land. But this is not a fearful thing for me, for my Father blesses me abundantly in the land and I lack no good thing.

n 1993, Richard Blackaby became president of a small seminary in Canada. Students were few, resources scarce, and facilities limited. But with mostly retired volunteer labor, they began building a new academic building.

On the morning the trusses were to be hung, an unusually forceful wind, even for the Rocky Mountain foothills, was blowing. The men had to hold onto their hats to keep them from blowing off. As the volunteers gathered to pray, they knew the situation was serious. It was too dangerous to hang the trusses with the wind blowing that way. But to delay hanging them would throw the volunteers' schedule into disarray.

At the close of the prayer time, the men stepped outside to an eerie calm. Not a trace of wind! For the next three days, while the trusses were hammered into place, not even a breeze was felt. As the last two trusses were hung, the wind returned; and as the last nail was hammered, the wind was back to full strength.

When you are faithful and obedient to the tasks that God has placed in your hands, He will give you the ability to finish those tasks with great success!

For the Lord your God has blessed you in
all the work of your hand. He knows your
walking through this great wilderness.
These forty years the Lord your God has
been with you; you have lacked nothing.

DEUTERONOMY 2:7 AMP

DECLARATION FOR YOUR LIFE

The Lord my God blesses all of the work of my hands.

was stumped. My old Macintosh laptop simply would not run the Mac Bible software anymore. Though I had worked with it for hours, nothing I did would help.

Finally, after having exhausted every last idea, I gave in and called the Mac Bible corporation. As I got on the phone, the person's name sounded familiar, and I soon learned why. The person on the line was none other than the man who wrote the Mac Bible software. He gave me a brief set of instructions, which, when I followed them, solved my problem. I just had to go to the man who wrote the program.

How many times do we try to work out our problems our own way instead of presenting them to the Lord? He promises to meet our needs. All we have to do is ask.

My God shall supply all your need according to his riches in glory by Christ Jesus.

PHILIPPIANS 4:19 KJV

DECLARATION FOR YOUR LIFE

When I present my offerings with the right heart attitude, they go up before the Lord like a sweet fragrance. I have God's word that He will supply all of my needs according to His riches in glory through Christ Jesus. He sees to it that all of my giving returns to me overflowing with His abundance.

ord, thank You for Your great provision which allows me to gain the blessing of wealth upon this earth. You have given me the power, the skill, the talents needed to produce wealth in my life here on earth. But even greater still, I thank You for the abundant life You give me both now and in my future home in heaven. You are a great God, and I bless You for all of the blessings You have given to me. In Jesus' name. Amen.

But thou shalt remember the Lord
thy God: for it is he that giveth thee
power to get wealth, that he may
establish his covenant which he sware
unto thy fathers, as it is this day.

DEUTERONOMY 8:18 KJV

DECLARATION FOR YOUR LIFE

*I am a wealth creator. Day and night I am given
unfailing ideas for the production of wealth in my life.
God expects me to take part in His gracious provision.
He wants me to have material things. It is the way I'm
supposed to live.*

ouston pastor John Bisagno describes a time when his daughter Melodye, age five, came to him and asked for a dollhouse. John promptly nodded, promised to build her one, and returned to his book. Soon he glanced out the window and saw her arms filled with dishes, toys, and dolls, making trip after trip until she had a great pile of playthings in the yard. When he asked his wife about it, she replied, "You promised to build her a dollhouse, and she believes you. She's just getting ready for it."

John threw aside his book, raced to the lumber-yard for supplies, and quickly built the dollhouse. Why? Because he wanted to? No. Because she deserved it? No. Her daddy had given his word, and she believed it and acted on it. When he saw her faith, nothing could keep him from carrying out his word.

Delight yourself in the Lord
  and he will give you the desires of
    your heart.
Commit your way to the Lord;
  trust in him and he will do this.

PSALM 37:4-5

DECLARATION FOR YOUR LIFE

The Lord is my comfort and my delight, and He gives me all the desires of my heart. My way is committed to Him, to trust in Him in every circumstance. He will make my righteousness shine like the dawn and the justice of my cause will blaze like the noonday sun.

harles Spurgeon was visiting an elderly woman in the almshouse. His attention was drawn to a framed document on the wall of her room, and he asked her about it. She said that years before, she had cared for an aged gentleman, and before he had died, he had written out a little note of appreciation to her followed by his signature. He had shortly afterwards died.

After much persuasion, Spurgeon was allowed to borrow the paper. When he took it to the bank, they exclaimed, "We've been wondering to whom the old gentleman left his money!" She was actually a wealthy woman, but she had been living like a beggar.[1]

God has supplied everything you need. Don't live like a beggar when you are rich in His kingdom.

The Lord will grant you abundant
prosperity—in the fruit of your womb,
the young of your livestock and the crops
of your ground—in the land he swore
to your forefathers to give you.

DEUTERONOMY 28:11

DECLARATION FOR YOUR LIFE

*The Lord gives me a tremendous surplus of prosperity
for my home and family. The fruit of my body, the
young of my cattle, and the produce of my ground are
blessed with His abundance.*

The King Is Home!

he king of a particular country traveled often, but one day a man living near the palace remarked to a friend, "Well, it looks like the king is home tonight."

"How do you know?" asked the other.

The man pointed up to the royal house. "Because when the king is home," he said, "the castle is all lit up."

Your body is the temple of the Holy Spirit, and the King is in residence there! Blessings and abundant prosperity are the demonstration to others that He is alive and well in your life. Don't be hesitant about telling others about the blessings in your life—you are a living example of the wonderful things God can do!

The Lord will open the heavens, the
storehouse of his bounty, to send rain
on your land in season and to bless all
the work of your hands. You will lend to
many nations but will borrow from none.

DEUTERONOMY 28:12

DECLARATION FOR YOUR LIFE

*My Lord gives rain to my land precisely when I need
it. He has opened to me His heavenly treasury. With
perfect timing He rains it down upon me and blesses
all the work of my hands.*

A Cheerful Heart

omposer Franz Joseph Haydn, recalling his struggles while working on a certain sacred work, wrote: "I prayed to God—not like a miserable sinner in despair—but calmly, slowly. In this I felt that an infinite God would surely have mercy on this finite creature. These thoughts cheered me up. I experienced a sure joy so confident that as I wished to express the prayer, I could not express my joy, but gave vent to my happy spirits and wrote the *Miserere*, 'Allegro.'"

Haydn's music was so ebullient in temperament that it was actually criticized by the sterner members of the church. His reply: "Since God has given me a cheerful heart, He will forgive me for serving Him cheerfully." When the blessings of God are poured out, there is not room to receive it—and great joy is the result!

The joy of the Lord is your strength.

NEHEMIAH 8:10

DECLARATION FOR YOUR LIFE

The joy of the Lord is my strength. It is both a shield and a weapon to me. It is a power force that withstands every attack of the enemy.

DELIGHT IN THE IMPOSSIBLE

ave you ever listened to children pray? Their faith knows no bounds. And who are the least surprised people when God answers prayers? The children.

But then we get older and grow too sophisticated for that. We use phrases such as, "Let's be realistic about this," or, "That may not be God's will." We lose that expectancy, that urgency of hope, that delightful, child-like, wide-eyed joy of faith. But God hasn't changed. As Saint Augustine once said, "God is more anxious to bestow His blessings on us than we are to receive them." God still delights in doing impossible things!

Nothing will be impossible with God.

LUKE 1:37 NASB

DECLARATION FOR YOUR LIFE

With God, the greater One who is within me, nothing is impossible. Every promise that He has given me has within it the power of fulfillment. Therefore, what He says I am, that is what I am; and what He says I can do, that is what I can do.

od has blessed us in so many ways. Psalm 103 says it all. This passage exhorts us to praise Him and to not forget all of His benefits. And what are some of these benefits?

He forgives all our sins.

He heals all our diseases.

He redeems our life from the pit.

He crowns us with love and compassion.

He satisfies us with good things.

He renews us day-by-day.

And all of these blessings come to us through Jesus and His sacrifice. We are truly blessed!

Blessed be the God and Father of our
Lord Jesus Christ, who hath blessed
us with all spiritual blessings in
heavenly places in Christ.

EPHESIANS 1:3 KJV

DECLARATION FOR YOUR LIFE

*I give all praise, honor, and glory to my God, the
Father of my Lord Jesus, for He has blessed me with
every spiritual blessing in Christ—including being a
part of His family.*

t was late, and Mark's young son, Peter, had been in bed for at least an hour. "Dad, can I have some ice cream?" the call came from his room.

"No, Peter, it's late, way past bedtime."

"But you promised!"

He was right. Peter had asked for some ice cream earlier in the day, but there wasn't any in the house. Mark had said, "I'll get some for you later, I promise."

Mark had forgotten all about the ice cream—but Peter hadn't. And so they found themselves at the convenience store buying ice cream after ten o'clock at night.

If human fathers know how to keep promises to their children—even when they forget—how much more will God keep each one of His great and precious promises to us! As A. W. Tozer once said, "The goodness of God is the drive behind all the blessings He daily bestows upon us."

If you, then, though you are evil, know how to give good gifts to your children, how much more will your Father in heaven give good gifts to those who ask him!

MATTHEW 7:11

DECLARATION FOR YOUR LIFE

My heavenly Father loves me and is always good to me. He is more than willing to give me specifically what I persistently ask for. When He sees that my heart is set on it, He makes sure that I have it.

Victory over Death

artin Luther, the Great Reformer, received many interesting blessings and answers to prayer in his lifetime. One of them occurred when Philip Melancthon, his closest friend, fell ill. Luther arrived at Philip's house to find him "about to give up the ghost. His eyes were set; his consciousness was almost gone; his speech had failed; he knew no one, and had ceased to take either solids or liquids."

Luther, beside himself with grief, exclaimed: "Blessed Lord, how has the devil spoiled me of this instrument!" He turned toward the window and began praying aloud earnestly. Almost instantly Philip began to move, and he was soon completely restored. He later said: "I should have been a dead man had I not been recalled from death itself by the coming of Luther."

God's grace will abound, His blessings will fall, when we speak forth His Word in our prayers!

Jesus said,… "I am the resurrection and the life. He who believes in Me, though he may die, he shall live."

JOHN 11:25 NKJV

DECLARATION FOR YOUR LIFE

Jesus is my resurrection and my life. All that I am is found in Him.

A Miraculous Healing

 page from the journal of John Wesley, the great evangelist and founder of the Methodist church:

"1741, May 10. Sunday, pain in back and head, with fever; had to lie down most of day; only easy in one position. At night, tried to preach; pain and seized with cough. There came to mind strongly, 'These signs shall follow them that believe.' Prayed; called on Jesus aloud to increase my faith and to confirm the Word of His grace. While I was speaking, my pain vanished away, the fever left me, my bodily strength returned, and for many weeks, I felt neither sickness nor pain. Unto Thee, O Lord, do I give thanks!"

Like John Wesley, by His stripes, you are healed this day!

He personally bore our sins in His [own] body on the tree [as on an altar and offered Himself on it], that we might die (cease to exist) to sin and live to righteousness. By His wounds you have been healed.

1 PETER 2:24 AMP

DECLARATION FOR YOUR LIFE

Jesus bore my sins in His own body while on the cross so that I might die to sin and live unto righteousness. Through His torment and agony, I was healed (cured; made whole).

harles Allen once said, "A hog will eat acorns under a tree day after day, never looking up to see where they came from. Some people are like that—but others are led through their blessings to realize the great love of their heavenly Father."

Are you a person who recognizes the blessings of God in your life? Or do you go through the day blindly taking advantage of your prosperity—in your soul, in your body, in your spirit?

God created us, and He wants us to be whole in every area of our lives. And He wants us to recognize Him for who He really is—the wonderful Gift-Giver who grants wonderful blessings to His children.

Beloved, I pray that you may prosper
in all things and be in health,
just as your soul prospers.

3 JOHN 2 NKJV

DECLARATION FOR YOUR LIFE

I know the heart of my Father—that He is a good Father, and wishes above all things that I prosper and remain healthy, even as my soul prospers.

GOD KEEPS HIS WORD!

here are four words that you must never forget: "God keeps His word." He doesn't tell us one thing and then do another. He doesn't, as we say, string us along. God doesn't lead us to believe something and then leave us in the lurch and let us down. God has veracity. God can be trusted. He operates in one realm, and that is the realm of truth.

The Bible says, "The Lord is good to all; he has compassion on all he has made" (Psalm 145:9). God's Word also tells us that none of the diseases of the world need befall the son or daughter of God (Exodus 15:26). God is the God who heals you. You can count on it!

If you will diligently hearken to the voice of the Lord your God and will do what is right in His sight, and will listen to and obey His commandments and keep all His statutes,
I will put none of the diseases upon you which I brought upon the Egyptians,
for I am the Lord Who heals you.

EXODUS 15:26 AMP

DECLARATION FOR YOUR LIFE

I have His word that no disease can come upon me which is brought upon the world; for my God is Jehovah Rapha, the God who heals me. He is the Lord of my health.

n 1680, after soldiers had dragged away her husband, William, because of his preaching, Marion Veitch said: *The Lord told me, "Trust in Me and fear not what man can do."* Shortly afterward news arrived that William was to be hanged. Marion rode on horseback through a blinding snowstorm to the jail, arriving at midnight. At daybreak, she was given a few last moments with her husband. The prosecutor, Thomas Bell, announced, "Veitch will hang tomorrow as he deserves."

That evening, Bell tarried at a friend's house, got drunk, and left after 10:00 PM His body was found the next morning, frozen in a ditch. Meanwhile, Veitch was pardoned at the last moment and lived a good long life with his wife by his side. In the end, God's blessings will overcome any evil that the world can bring.

You are of God, little children, and have overcome them, because He who is in you is greater than he who is in the world.

1 JOHN 4:4 NKJV

DECLARATION FOR YOUR LIFE

I am of God and have already defeated and overcome Satan, devils, and all spirits of Antichrist, because greater is He who is in me than he who is in the world.

You Can Do All Things!

here is something wonderfully exciting about reaching into the future with excited anticipation—knowing that God will enable you to do all things through Him. In fact, those who pursue new adventures in Him will stay younger, think better, and laugh louder than anyone else! Mark, who is in his mid-fifties, smiles from ear to ear as he tells of his plans to teach himself Mandarin, one of the Chinese dialects, so that he can be fluent in the language when he leaves for Mongolia as a missionary.

What is it that God is calling you to do? Whatever it is, He will give you the strength, the talent, the gifting—and the opportunity—to do it and do it well!

I have strength for all things in Christ
Who empowers me [I am ready for
anything and equal to anything through
Him Who infuses inner strength into me;
I am self-sufficient in Christ's sufficiency].

PHILIPPIANS 4:13 AMP

DECLARATION FOR YOUR LIFE

*The secret is this: I can do all things through the power
of Christ that is within me. With His anointing, there
isn't a single circumstance that can hold me down! I
am self-sufficient in His sufficiency.*

GOD'S PROMISES ARE ALL YOU NEED

 od's promises are real and true—more real than any problem you could ever face.

Hudson Taylor, the famous missionary to China in the 19th century, when faced with a time of poverty and lack in the work of China's Inland Mission, turned to his wife and said, "All we have left is twenty-five cents—and all of the promises of God!" Charles H. Spurgeon also remarked: "I have thumbed my Bible many a year. I have never yet thumbed a broken promise. The promises have all been kept to me; not one good thing has failed."

God's intent for you is blessing, not harm, and He promises to satisfy your mouth with *good things*.

Who satisfieth thy mouth with good things;
so that thy youth is renewed like the eagle's.

PSALM 103:5 KJV

DECLARATION FOR YOUR LIFE

*He satisfies my every desire with good things so that
my youth is renewed within me, and that I may soar
into this life like an eagle on the wing.*

LITTLE JOYS

im Elliot, the martyred missionary to the Auca Indians of Ecuador, wrote to his wife, Elisabeth, before his death: "Amy Carmichael writes of little joys, like flowers springing up by the path unnoticed except by those who are looking for them. Little things, like a quietly sinking sun, a friendly dog, a ready smile. We sang a little song in kindergarten which I've never forgotten: 'The world is so full of a number of things/I'm sure we should all be as happy as kings.' Simple, but I am impressed with the joy that is ours in Christ, so that heaven above and earth below become brighter and fairer."[2]

Thank God today for the blessings that are yours in Christ!

If they obey and serve him, they shall
spend their days in prosperity,
and their years in pleasures.

JOB 36:11 KJV

DECLARATION FOR YOUR LIFE

*The Lord sets me back on the path of His prosperity and
sees to it that I spend my days in peace and contentment.*

ometimes we must decide to be happy. But when we choose to recognize God's blessings in our lives, His joy will be ours. The Lord dwells in joy, and He makes Himself at home in a heart that is happy.

God is the Giver of the greatest joy that you will ever know. When you make Him the Lord of your life, He can work within you to fill you with unspeakable joy. All you need to do is ask Him in and allow His blessings to pour down upon you. When you are truly filled with joy, the whole world will see it. They will notice that you are not like everyone else, and there is no more powerful testimony to the power of God than a smile that cannot be taken away.

May those who delight in my vindication
    shout for joy and gladness;
may they always say, "The Lord be exalted,
    who delights in the well-being of
        his servant."

PSALM 35:27

DECLARATION FOR YOUR LIFE

*The Lord delights in the abundance of my prosperity,
and I shout for joy because of the blessings that He
brings! I will exalt His name forever!*

NO ROOM FOR WORRY

hen you are speaking God's Word continually, there is no room for worry or doubt to fill your mind. And as you hear God's Word and build up your faith in Him, He will be able to work out His will for prosperity and good success in a greater and greater way in your life. Commit to speaking the Word and pushing worry aside. There is nothing you will ever face that you and God, together, can't handle. Turn your worries over to God and let Him handle them. He has your best interests at heart!

This book of the law shall not depart out of thy mouth; but thou shalt meditate therein day and night, that thou mayest observe to do according to all that is written therein: for then thou shalt make thy way prosperous, and then thou shalt have good success.

Joshua 1:8 kjv

Declaration for Your Life

I speak the Word continually. I meditate upon it day and night so that I may do all that is written therein. By this, I make my way prosperous, have good success, and deal wisely in all of the affairs of my life.

uring the Great Depression, two families shared a house in Pennsylvania. One family occupied the upper floor, and the other family lived on the lower. The family which lived downstairs was always inviting people to share what they had. When there was an opportunity for them to give, they always seemed to have enough. The family on the upper floor, however, scoffed at the way the downstairs family lived. They stored all of their extras in a locker in the pantry. They gave nothing away. It was not until they found that rats had gotten into their pantry that they were sad about what they had done. Interestingly, the rats had not disturbed the downstairs pantry!

When we put God's kingdom first, God will bless us, and the blessing will be double because of the joy that it brings.

Seek first his kingdom and his
righteousness, and all these things
will be given to you as well.

MATTHEW 6:33

DECLARATION FOR YOUR LIFE

*My first thought in all things is the advancement of
the kingdom and God's way of being and doing
things. With this mindset and spiritual stronghold, all
of my physical and material needs will shower into
my life in a flood of abundance.*

cardiologist created a stir with a research study on the benefits of prayer. He had volunteers pray for one group of patients while another group served as a control. Those in the prayed-for group were five times less likely to require antibiotics or ventilators. The doctor concluded: "The evidence strongly suggests faith in God is truly linked to a long, healthy life."

A German proverb states: "When in prayer you clasp your hands, God opens His." Whatever is on your heart, when you make your requests known to your Father, He will wholeheartedly meet all of your needs.

[The Lord] will surely be gracious to you at the sound of your cry; when He hears it, He will answer you.

ISAIAH 30:19 NASB

DECLARATION FOR YOUR LIFE

The Lord is generous and loving toward me when I call out to Him, and He is quick to respond when I need His help.

ance Havner once wrote:

God is faithful, and He expects His people to be faithful. God's Word speaks of faithful servants, faithful in a few things, faithful in the Lord, faithful ministers. And all point to that day when He will say, "Well done, thou good and faithful servant." True faith shows up in faithfulness. Not everyone can sing or preach, but all can be faithful.[5]

When you are faithful, all of God's blessings will abound toward you.

A faithful man shall abound with blessings.

PROVERBS 28:20 KJV

DECLARATION FOR YOUR LIFE

*I am a faithful and industrious man/woman, and
God blesses and prospers all that I set my hand to do.*

ne of the great themes of Christianity is triumphant hope. Not just hope as in a distant, vague dream, but triumphant hope, the kind of hope where all things end right. In the midst of the struggles and the storms and the sufferings of life, we can advance our thoughts beyond today and see all of the blessings that God has awaiting us.

Through the prophet Isaiah, God declared, "I am the Lord your God, who upholds your right hand, Who says to you, 'Do not fear; I will help you'" (Isaiah 41:13 NASB). Thank God that He is ready, able, and willing to help you this day as you keep His Word on your lips and triumphant faith and hope in your heart!

"I, your GOD, have a firm grip on you and I'm not letting go. I'm telling you, 'Don't panic. I'm right here to help you.'"

ISAIAH 41:13 THE MESSAGE

DECLARATION FOR YOUR LIFE

The Lord says to me, "Son/Daughter, don't you worry about a thing. I've got your back and won't let anything harm you. I'm always here for you to help you with anything you need. So don't be afraid."

ll of us have our own particular fears. Fear of darkness. Fear of failure. Fear of the unknown. Fear of heights. Fear of financial disaster. Fear of sickness. Fear of death. You name it, we entertain it. Yet God promises to deliver us from all our fears, and so it stands to reason that we can rest in Him. He shields us when we take refuge in Him.

God will lift you up from the horrible pit and place your feet on a rock. He will prove Himself strong in your weakness and give you the authority to trample all of Satan's schemes in your life. Thank God that we have the power to overcome anything we face, in Jesus' name!

Behold, I give unto you power to tread on serpents and scorpions, and over all the power of the enemy: and nothing shall by any means hurt you.

LUKE 10:19 KJV

DECLARATION FOR YOUR LIFE

I have all of the authority that I need to trample down serpents and scorpions and I have mental, physical, and spiritual strength over and above all that the enemy possesses. There is nothing that Satan can do to harm me in any way.

ship was wrecked in a furious storm and the only survivor was a little boy who was swept by the waves onto a rock. He sat there all night long until, the next morning, he was spotted and rescued. "Did you tremble while you were on the rock during the night?" someone later asked him.

"Yes," said the boy. "I trembled all night—but the rock didn't."

God personally cares about the things that worry us—and He offers us His peace in the midst of the storm. First Peter 5:7 invites you to "cast all your anxiety on him because he cares for you." He cares. You are His personal concern. Rest in His peace.

You will keep him in perfect peace,
Whose mind is stayed on You,
Because he trusts in You.

ISAIAH 26:3 NKJV

DECLARATION FOR YOUR LIFE

*My mind is steadfast, trusting in the Lord, and He keeps
me in perfect peace. I am committed to the Lord forever.*

As a result of God's mercy, we have become a people who are uniquely and exclusively cared for by God. The fact that we are the recipients of His mercy makes all the difference in the world as to how our plans will turn out. When we commit all of our works and our ways to Him, we will have great success. God watches over us with enormous interest, waiting to perform His Word in our lives. What encouraging news!

What "works" are you committing to the Lord this day? Rest assured, as you follow Him and His plans for your life, you will have great success!

Commit thy works unto the Lord,
and thy thoughts shall be established.

PROVERBS 16:3 KJV

DECLARATION FOR YOUR LIFE

I commit my way to the Lord. Everything that I do is covered and saturated with His mercy, and all of my plans are destined to succeed.

little girl once broke one of her mother's treasured teacups. She came to her mother sobbing, "Oh, Mama, I'm so sorry I broke your beautiful cup."

The mother replied, "I know you're sorry, and I forgive you. Don't cry anymore." The mother swept up the pieces of the broken cup and placed them in the trash. But then the girl went to the trash can, picked up the pieces of the cup, brought them to her mother and sobbed, "Mother, I'm so sorry I broke your pretty cup."

This time her mother spoke firmly to her, "Take those pieces and put them back in the trash and don't be silly enough to take them out again. I told you I forgive you!"

When God forgives you, He forgets about what you have done and doesn't bring it up again. What a blessing it is to be forgiven by Him!

Blessed are they whose iniquities are forgiven, and whose sins are covered.

ROMANS 4:7 KJV

DECLARATION FOR YOUR LIFE

Jesus has justified me through my faith and He Himself has become my righteousness. Even David spoke of this righteousness that I now enjoy, saying, "Blessed is the one whose iniquities are forgiven and whose sins have been completely eradicated."

ed McDonough, who lives in New South Wales, one day noticed in his neighbor's trash bin a small New Testament in very good condition. Ted was not a "religious" man, but he picked it up, saying to himself, *You're too good to be thrown away.* And he put the book in his pocket.

Years later, when Ted's personal life and marriage problems caused him to question the meaning of life, he decided to go to church. So, one Sunday morning, he got up early, dressed carefully, and went off to the local church. Ted lived in a small town and the Christians did not have church every week, and the church doors were shut. He went home and hunted for and found the New Testament he had picked up from the trash years earlier. In its pages, Ted found forgiveness, guidance, and a new life.

When we trust in its truths, God's Word will be a light unto our path.

Your word is a lamp to my feet
And a light to my path.

PSALM 119:105 NKJV

DECLARATION FOR YOUR LIFE

God's Word is a lamp unto my feet and a light unto my path. It guides me in every decision I need to make and helps me see the right way to go.

GUIDED BY HIS HAND

hen Anne Graham Lotz and her husband, Danny, attend football games at his alma mater, the University of North Carolina, thousands of people cram into the parking lots, and she can't see where she's going. However, her husband, a head taller at 6'7", can look over the crowd, so he takes her hand and leads them to their seats.

"The way I get from the car to my seat is by holding his hand and following him closely through the crowd," she says.

She follows the same procedure with the Lord. "I just try to faithfully follow the Lord step-by-step and day by day. Ten years from now, I just want to look back and know that to the best of my ability I have been obedient to God's call on my life."[4]

When you follow the path God calls you to follow, you will be blessed by Him.

The path of the righteous is like the first
  gleam of dawn,
shining ever brighter till the full light of day.

PROVERBS 4:18

DECLARATION FOR YOUR LIFE

*The path the Lord has laid before me is as a shining
light that shines more and more unto a perfect day.*

od has a master plan for your life and that plan does not change. It is a plan designed specifically for you. It is a plan that God intends for you to live out fully, beginning at the moment of your birth and continuing on until the moment you go on to be with the Lord in heaven. God's plan for you has a purpose, a blueprint for your particular life, a guidance plan, and a plan for blessing you. Your destiny is to be the person God has created you to be.

Trust God to show you the plan He has for your life. When you follow His plan and His way, blessings will follow.

Trust in the Lord with all thine heart; and
lean not unto thine own understanding.
In all thy ways acknowledge him,
and he shall direct thy paths.

PROVERBS 3:5–6 KJV

DECLARATION FOR YOUR LIFE

*I give my whole heart to trust in the Lord. I will not be
the fool who balances his life on the brace of human
understanding. I am God-inside minded at all times
and never cease to acknowledge His presence to guide
me in all that I do. He sees what I cannot see and
knows what I do not know. With Him at the point, all
of my paths are made straight. Therefore, I will never
put my own wisdom before the Lord's.*

COMPLETE IN HIM

 e are complete in Jesus Christ. In Him we are made ready, we are equipped, for any crisis or circumstance that may come.

The children of Israel wandered in a wilderness, but their shoes didn't wear out, even though they wandered there for forty years. When the children of Israel needed water, God supplied it. When they needed food, He sent manna. When they needed guidance, He gave them a very clear and present witness to lead them by day and by night. When they were surrounded by enemies, He delivered them. His means were sovereign and supernatural, and His provision was complete and sure.

You can trust the Lord to do the same for you.

Ye are complete in [Christ].

COLOSSIANS 2:10 KJV

DECLARATION FOR YOUR LIFE

In Christ all the fullness of the Godhead dwells in bodily form, and through my identification with Him I have been given that very same fullness.

arry Hoffman went to a Goodwill store in Wisconsin looking for a bargain. He found one. Larry picked out a shirt, paid for it, and took it home. However, when he tried it on, Larry discovered the shirt was too small for him. And then Larry found something else. Stuffed in the pocket of the shirt was a wad of cash totaling $2,000.

Larry took the money to the police station, but because no one claimed it, it ultimately was given back to Larry. It was an amazing blessing—and completely unexpected.

God loves to surprise His chosen ones with unexpected blessings.

These all wait for You,
That You may give them their food in
    due season.
What You give them they gather in;
You open Your hand, they are filled
    with good.

PSALM 104:27-28 NKJV

DECLARATION FOR YOUR LIFE

*God answers my every prayer. His hand is open to me
and my harvest overflows with good things.*

You Are Valuable!

number of people are told from child-hood, "You'll never amount to anything." What a terrible message regarding a person's worthiness or value.

The truth of God is what that person needs to hear! God says that you *do* amount to something. You are so valuable that God desires to live with you forever!

God says that you are a special person. You are so special and valuable that He sent His Son, Jesus Christ, to die for your sins, and He made it possible for the Holy Spirit to come and dwell within you to remind you on a daily basis that you are a somebody in His eyes. You are valuable beyond measure to God!

For I know the thoughts that I think toward you, saith the Lord, thoughts of peace, and not of evil, to give you an expected end.

JEREMIAH 29:11 KJV

DECLARATION FOR YOUR LIFE

All of God's thoughts for me are for good and never evil. His plan for my life is to make me prosperous, give me hope, and provide for me a glorious future. He has handpicked everything that is best for me in life and presents it to me with great joy. His desire for me is to live in His abundance.

GOD'S HANDS ARE BIGGER

 young boy went to the local candy store with his mother. The shop owner, a kindly old man, passed him a large jar of lollipops and invited him to help himself to a handful. When the boy said no, the shopkeeper reached in and pulled out a handful for the boy.

When outside, the boy's mother asked why he had suddenly been so shy and wouldn't reach into the jar when the man had offered.

The boy replied, "Because his hands are so much bigger than mine!" The man was able to hold a greater amount of candy than the boy ever could.

God's hands are so much bigger than ours! Allow Him to bless you in the ways He sees fit and you'll be surprised at how "pleasant" your inheritance will be.

Trust in the Lord, and do good;
so shalt thou dwell in the land,
and verily thou shalt be fed.

PSALM 37:3 KJV

DECLARATION FOR YOUR LIFE

My purposes are set in the Lord to dwell in His spacious lands and enjoy the abundance of His pastures. I stand for what is good and right, and trust in Him with unfailing loyalty. He is my comfort and my delight, and He gives me all the desires of my heart.

The Blessing of Peace

he Greek word for *peace* means "to bind together" something that has been broken or disjointed. This is a superb illustration for how alienated men and women—so often feeling empty and disconnected from each other and God—can find a way to unity and wholeness. God's peace comes to them when they are united by faith in God.

This Greek word also refers to a prevailing sense of quietness and rest in a person's heart and emotions—of being unperturbed and unruffled. Peace is synonymous with being tranquil, serene, untroubled, and calm.

One of God's greatest blessings is His peace!

Be careful for nothing; but in every thing by
prayer and supplication with thanksgiving
let your requests be made known unto God.
And the peace of God, which passeth all
understanding, shall keep your hearts
and minds through Christ Jesus.

PHILIPPIANS 4:6–7 KJV

DECLARATION FOR YOUR LIFE

*The Lord is very near to me. No matter what situation
I find myself in, I have a loving heavenly Father who
will intervene on my behalf. When I present my prayers
and petitions to Him, with thanksgiving, He causes
everything to work together for my good. The peace of
God, which is beyond human understanding, guards
my heart and my mind in Christ Jesus.*

LIFE IN THE DESERT

eath Valley may no longer deserve its name. Normally the hottest and driest place in North America, in 2005 this desert area in California experienced the wettest year in a century. As a result, colorful wildflowers are in bloom. Vast fields of desert gold poppy, desert star, and evening primrose have sprouted in the usually barren moonscape, which includes the lowest point in the Western Hemisphere.

Heavy rains have resulted in flooding and mudslides elsewhere in California, but the rainwater has brought the desert to life. Referring to the explosion of color, one reporter said, "2005 is a year likely to be remembered as the wildflower show of a lifetime."

Just as God has brought life to the desert of California, He can bring renewal and abundance to the desert areas of your life.

[The Lord says], I will set in the desert the
fir tree, and the pine, and the box tree
together: That they may see, and know,
and consider, and understand together, that
the hand of the Lord hath done this, and
the Holy One of Israel hath created it.

ISAIAH 41:19-20 KJV

DECLARATION FOR YOUR LIFE

The Lord says to me, "I will make rivers flow on your
barren heights and turn your desert places into pools
of water. All that you have I will bless for your sake."

lthough God cares about financial stability, world peace, and social justice, He has one great thing on His mind today—you. You are His workmanship, His masterpiece (see Ephesians 2:10). He has planned all of your steps for this very day!

There is no one else in the world exactly like you, and God cares for you with infinite watchfulness. He knows exactly how many hairs came out in your brush this morning. Your checkbook matters to Him as much as the federal budget, and harmony in your home is as important to Him as harmony among nations.

One of the greatest blessings of being a child of God is having your life be His greatest concern!

The steps of a good man are ordered by
the Lord: and he delighteth in his way.

PSALM 37:23 KJV

DECLARATION FOR YOUR LIFE

*My Father is overjoyed to spend His time with me. He
rejoices as we walk this life together, and He sees to it
that all of my steps stand firm.*

od will not withhold anything from you that is rightfully yours as His child.

God will not hide any aspect of His character from you.

God will not deny you any promise that He makes in His Word.

God will not shut you away from any blessing that is for your eternal benefit or that is required for the fulfillment of your purpose on this earth.

And best of all, God has already prepared for you all that you will need for every day of the rest of your life.

Thou wilt shew me the path of life: in thy presence is fulness of joy; at thy right hand there are pleasures for evermore.

PSALM 16:11 KJV

DECLARATION FOR YOUR LIFE

What a joy it is to be a child of God! My heart leaps within me and my tongue rejoices in His praise! I am raised with Jesus and shall never be abandoned to hell. He has made known to me the path of life and fills me with joy in His presence. At His right hand, I shall have abundant pleasures for all of eternity.

hen Jerome Groopman diagnosed patients with serious diseases, the Harvard medical school professor discovered that all of them were "looking for a sense of genuine hope, and indeed, that hope was as important to them as anything he might prescribe as a physician."

When asked for his definition of *hope*, he replied: "Basically, I think hope is the ability to see a path to the future. You are facing dire circumstances, and you need to know everything that's blocking or threatening you. And then you see a path, or a potential path, to get where you want to be."

The doctor confessed: "I think hope has been, is, and always will be, the heart of medicine and healing. We could not live without hope." In what do you place your hope today? When you hope in God's mercy, you will never be disappointed.

For His anger is but for a moment,
His favor is for life;
Weeping may endure for a night,
But joy comes in the morning.

PSALM 30:5 NKJV

DECLARATION FOR YOUR LIFE

*His anger lasts only a moment, but His favor and
abundance of blessings last a lifetime. I may weep
during the night, but He will raise me up with rejoicing in the morning.*

he famous missionary C. T. Studd once traveled to China on a ship whose captain was an embittered opponent of Christianity and who often studied the Bible for the sole purpose of arguing with the missionaries who frequently sailed on his ship. When he learned that Studd was onboard his ship, the captain lit into him. But instead of arguing with him, Studd put his arm around the captain and said, "But, my friend, I have a peace that passeth all understanding and a joy that nothing can take away."

The captain finally replied, "You're a lucky dog," and walked away. Before the end of the voyage, he became a rejoicing believer in Jesus Christ.[5]

I am not ashamed of the gospel of Christ:
for it is the power of God unto salvation
to every one that believeth.

ROMANS 1:16 KJV

DECLARATION FOR YOUR LIFE

*I am not ashamed of the Gospel of Jesus Christ. I share
it with people wherever I go.*

ave you ever noticed how trusting kids are? When we are young, we believe and trust so easily. But along come hurts, betrayals, and life's tragedies, and suddenly we aren't so trusting anymore. We become fearful and build walls around ourselves in a vain effort to prevent future hurt. But then, God enters the picture. He tells us of a new way to deal with life's cares. Instead of giving in to fear, He tells us to believe that He is with us.

Take the time to consider that He is with you—right now—in this very moment. He is pure love; so, we can trust Him. He has promised to help us, and because He is all-powerful, He can and He will! We need to let go of our fear and cling to Him. He will be there waiting.

Do not fear, for I am with you;
  do not be dismayed, for I am your God.
I will strengthen you and help you;
  I will uphold you with my righteous
    right hand.

ISAIAH 41:10

DECLARATION FOR YOUR LIFE

I have no cause for fear, for my God is with me. I will not be dismayed, for God is my Father and He has promised to never leave me nor forsake me. He strengthens me and assists me in every circumstance. He upholds me with His righteous right hand so that my victory is made certain.

o's five-year-old daughter, Barbara, had disobeyed her and been sent to her room. After a few minutes, Jo went in to talk with her about what she had done. Teary-eyed, she asked, "Why do we do wrong things, Mommy?"

"Well," Jo replied, "sometimes the devil tells us to do something wrong and we listen to him. We need to listen to God instead."

To which the daughter sobbed, "But God doesn't talk loud enough!"

God *does* talk loud enough—when we choose to listen. And when we choose to listen, He promises to bless us abundantly.

Walk in all the way that the Lord your God
has commanded you, so that you may
live and prosper and prolong your days
in the land that you will possess.

DEUTERONOMY 5:33

DECLARATION FOR YOUR LIFE

I walk in all of the ways of God. He is my Mentor and
the example by which I live. I obey His every command.
His Word is life to me, and I will obey it so that it may
go well with me and that I may live long in the land
that He has given me.

arty Johnson knew he was the product of two young college students who had had a brief affair. Neither parent was prepared to deal with raising a child, so he was given up for adoption and grew up in a loving home in Minnesota. Years later, as an adult, he started digging through past records and got in touch with his birth mother.

Then one day a letter arrived that said, "Welcome to the Ogike dynasty! You come from a noble and prestigious family." The letter went on to explain that Johnson was next in line to inherit the position of village chief from his biological father, John Ogike.

In a similar way, we have been adopted into the kingdom of God as His children and heirs to all of His blessings. Because of Him, we lack nothing!

The God of heaven will prosper us.

NEHEMIAH 2:20 AMP

DECLARATION FOR YOUR LIFE

My Father grants me success in all that I set my hand to do. He bids me to lay claim to my rightful inheritance in this earth.

arilyn wrote to a close friend explaining that she had problems sleeping at night. When her next letter arrived, she learned that her friend had problems sleeping as well, but she used her wakefulness to pray for loved ones, listing her concerns alphabetically by first names. Now, as Marilyn drifts off, lovingly praying for Adriana, Alan, Amelia, and Amy, she feels surrounded by loved ones and she smiles. She's not just counting sheep— she's counting *His* sheep.

The Lord promises sweet sleep to His children. If you have trouble sleeping in the peace that He has promised to you, try praying for loved ones or counting His blessings to you. Rest safe and secure in His arms, and receive the sleep He has assured.

I will both lie down in peace, and sleep;
For You alone, O Lord, make me dwell
in safety.

PSALM 4:8 NKJV

DECLARATION FOR YOUR LIFE

I will lie down and sleep in perfect peace—safe and secure in the arms of my heavenly Father.

here once was a Peanuts cartoon in which Lucy said to Charlie Brown: "I hate everything. I hate everybody. I hate the whole wide world!"

Charlie Brown protested: "But I thought you had inner peace."

Lucy replied, "I do have inner peace. But I still have outer obnoxiousness!"

How many Christians are still living like Lucy? God promises His inner peace when the Holy Spirit fills our lives—and we commit to set our outer obnoxiousness aside! His Word promises that when you choose to live according to His Word, in ways that are pleasing to Him, He will bring both inner—and outer—peace to your life.

When a man's ways please the Lord,
He makes even his enemies to
be at peace with him.

PROVERBS 16:7 NKJV

DECLARATION FOR YOUR LIFE

I choose to live in ways that are pleasing to the Lord,
and He makes even my enemies to be at peace with me.

E. Marsh once listed just a few of the many blessings God pours out on His children:

An acceptance that can never be questioned (Ephesians 1:6).

An inheritance that can never be lost (1 Peter 1:3–5).

A deliverance that can never be excelled (2 Corinthians 1:10).

A grace that can never be limited (2 Corinthians 12:9).

A hope that can never be disappointed (Hebrews 6:18–19).

A joy that can never be diminished (John 15:11).

A peace that can never be disturbed (John 14:27).

A righteousness that can never be tarnished (2 Corinthians 5:21).

A salvation that can never be canceled (Hebrews 5:9).[6]

You can be sure that God will take
care of everything you need.

PHILIPPIANS 4:19 THE MESSAGE

DECLARATION FOR YOUR LIFE

In Jesus, I have everything I need.

A father watched through the kitchen window as his small son attempted to lift a large stone out of his sandbox. The boy was frustrated as he wrestled with the heavy object because he just couldn't get enough leverage to lift it over the side. Finally the boy gave up and sat down dejectedly on the edge of the sandbox with his head in his hands.

The father went outside and asked, "What's wrong, Son? Can't you lift that rock out of the sandbox?"

"No, sir," the boy said, "I can't do it."

"Have you used all the strength that's available to you?" the father asked.

"Yes, sir," the boy replied.

"No, you haven't," the father said. "You haven't asked me to help you."

As His beloved children, God's abundant power is available to help us in any and all of life's circumstances.

God is our refuge and strength,
A very present help in trouble.

PSALM 46:1 NKJV

DECLARATION FOR YOUR LIFE

God is my refuge and the power that sustains me. He is my ever-present help in time of need.

Blessed with Forgiveness

uring the Great Awakening, when the Spirit of God revived much of our nation's early faith, Jonathan Edwards was presiding over a massive prayer meeting. Eight hundred men prayed with him.

Into that meeting a woman sent another woman with a note, asking the men to pray for her husband. The note described a man who had become unloving, prideful, and difficult.

Edwards read the message in private and then, thinking that perhaps the man described was present, made a bold request. Edwards read the note to the eight hundred men. Then he asked if the man who had been described would raise his hand so that the whole assembly could pray for him. Three hundred men raised their hands.

When you confess your sins, the Lord is faithful and just to forgive you your sins and cleanse you from all unrighteousness. That is one of His greatest blessings!

Blessed is he

   whose transgressions are forgiven,

   whose sins are covered.

   PSALM 32:1

DECLARATION FOR YOUR LIFE

I am blessed, for the Lord has forgiven all of my transgressions and has eliminated every sin that was set to my account.

he psalmist tells us that when we ask God to forgive our sins, He removes them as far as the east is from the west. Do you know how far that is? The truth is, it can't even be measured.

If you look at a globe, you will be able to see that the east and west are actually farther apart than the north and the south. If you start in North America and travel north, eventually you will reach the top of the globe at the North Pole. And if you continue going the same direction, you start going south. Eventually the north meets the south.

But if you start in North America and keep going east, when will you ever start going west? Never! The psalmist says that God will remove our sin from us— not as far as the north is from the south, but as far as the east is from the west—as far away as we could ever comprehend.

As far as the east is from the west, so far hath he removed our transgressions from us.

PSALM 103:12 KJV

DECLARATION FOR YOUR LIFE

God does not punish me like my sins deserve or repay me according to the evil things that I have done. For as high as the heavens are above the earth, so great is His love for me. As far as the east is from the west, so far has He removed all of my sins from me. They will never be brought up again.

The Icing on the Cake

 auri took her sons, twelve-year-old Matthew and six-year-old Ryan, to her parents' house for an afternoon visit. They spent some time playing and socializing with their grandparents. When they were ready to leave, Lauri's dad said to Matthew, "You made my day."

Matthew replied: "God made your day; we just put the icing on it."

One of God's greatest blessings is the relationships that we establish with our friends and family here on earth. They are the "icing" on the "cake" of life!

Every desirable and beneficial gift comes
out of heaven. The gifts are rivers of light
cascading down from the Father of Light.

JAMES 1:17 THE MESSAGE

DECLARATION FOR YOUR LIFE

*I know that every good and perfect gift comes from my
heavenly Father, the Father of heavenly lights.*

he departure area for Paul's flight was buzzing with stern-looking men in dark suits talking into their lapels. He asked a flight attendant what was happening. She replied, "Just wait. You'll see."

After he settled into his economy-class seat, two of the dark-suited men arrived in first class, followed by former president Gerald Ford. He was sitting a few rows away! *I've never met a president before! I'll go introduce myself,* he thought. But then he wondered, *Why would he want to meet me?* Then he remembered that during his years in seminary, he had met President Ford's son, Mike. So Paul marched into first class. Before the Secret Service could stop him, he said: "President Ford, I know your son, Mike." They talked briefly, mostly about Mike. Mike's name gave Paul "authority" to approach the former president.

In the same way, Jesus' name gives us the blessing of approaching the Father boldly and without fear.

Let us therefore come boldly unto the throne of grace, that we may obtain mercy, and find grace to help in time of need.

HEBREWS 4:16 KJV

DECLARATION FOR YOUR LIFE

In Jesus, the way has been opened for me to freely receive God's help in any and every circumstance I find myself in. I can approach God with confidence!

Persistence Pays Off

writer in his fifties had written a manuscript for a book and had sent it off to several publishers without success. He grew so discouraged that he threw the manuscript into the wastepaper basket. But his wife decided to show the manuscript to one more publisher. And when the editor read it, he loved it.

The writer in this story is Norman Vincent Peale; the manuscript was *The Power of Positive Thinking.* The book that Peale tossed in the trash can eventually sold thirty million copies.

God's blessings come to those who persevere and keep their faith strong. Don't give up on the vision God has given you—you may be just one step away from success!

Let us not be weary in well doing: for in due season we shall reap, if we faint not.

GALATIANS 6:9 KJV

DECLARATION FOR YOUR LIFE

I purpose in my heart to never become weary in doing good, for at the proper time I will reap an abundant harvest as long as I do not give up.

gnes's granddaughter, Hannah, begged her long-distance over the phone to come help her celebrate her sixth birthday. Unable to resist, Agnes made her plans to join the family.

When they sat down for the birthday dinner, Agnes's son asked Hannah if she would like to bless the food on her birthday. "Oh yes, Daddy," she said.

She closed her eyes and began, "Dear Lord, thank You for Mommy and this good food she fixed. Thank You for letting Grandma come here today."

Pausing momentarily, Hannah opened her eyes to peek at her grandmother before she continued, "And please, Lord, let us have a good time at Toys R Us this afternoon!"

The boldness Hannah displayed was based on her relationship with her grandmother. That same boldness can be ours when we realize that, through Jesus, we can approach the throne of the Father and ask that His blessings become ours.

Therefore...we have confidence to enter the Most Holy Place by the blood of Jesus.

HEBREWS 10:19

DECLARATION FOR YOUR LIFE

By Him, I can now approach the very throne of God, the throne of grace, with boldness and confidence, without the slightest sense of inadequacy whatsoever, so that I can obtain His mercy and supernatural ability to help me in my time of need.

hil Callaway didn't know what to say when his young children asked if Mommy was going to die. His wife, Ramona, suffered horrible seizures.

Hundreds of friends and relatives prayed, but Ramona's weight eventually slipped to ninety pounds. Medical specialists tried everything, but by the fall of 1996, the seizures were occurring daily, sometimes hourly.

Phil rarely left Ramona's side. He wondered if she would even make it to her thirtieth birthday. One evening when things looked totally hopeless, Phil paced their dark backyard, then fell to his knees. "God!" he cried out. "I can't take it anymore. Please do something!"

Suddenly a doctor's name came to mind. Phil called the doctor, who saw Ramona the next morning and diagnosed a rare chemical deficiency.

Within a week, Ramona's seizures ended. Her eyes sparkled again. The miracle was so incredible that Phil said, "God Himself gave me back my wife!"

Jesus said unto him, If thou canst believe,
all things are possible to him that believeth.

MARK 9:23 KJV

DECLARATION FOR YOUR LIFE

I believe in God's power and ability within me.
Therefore, all things are possible for me.

other eagles are caring and loving creatures, but at some point, she must decide her little eaglet needs to learn to fly. So she takes it out of the nest and flies up as high in the air as she can go. At that point, she drops the fledgling, and he falls fast. The eaglet has never flown in his life. The ground is coming up, his heart is ready to burst, and he knows there is no way he is going to survive.

But the mother eagle is watching, and at the last moment, she swoops down and catches the baby eaglet. She continues to follow this process until the eaglet has learned how to fly.

The Lord will bear you up on eagles' wings. Even if you feel like you are falling, remember, you're actually learning how to fly.

[The Lord says], "I carried you on eagles' wings and brought you to myself. Now if you obey me fully and keep my covenant, then out of all nations you will be my treasured possession."

EXODUS 19:4

DECLARATION FOR YOUR LIFE

The Lord has delivered me from my enemies. He bore me on eagles' wings and brought me unto Himself. I have been reconciled unto almighty God!

ears ago, Mike had a hobby of collecting baseball cards. He collected favorite players and teams and occasionally some which were for investment. But as he began college, his hobby was replaced with other ways to spend money.

On a whim, he recently purchased a pack of inexpensive cards and was amazed to discover one of the rarest cards of the set sitting there in his hand. It even had a real autograph on it. When the shock of the moment wore off, he realized that he had found something he would have paid hundreds of dollars for if he had not found it in a five-dollar pack of cards.

God's blessings often come to us like that. When we follow His ways, He will surprise us by giving us the desires of our heart—and more.

Blessings are upon the head of the [uncompromisingly] righteous (the upright, in right standing with God) but the mouth of the wicked conceals violence.

PROVERBS 10:6 AMP

DECLARATION FOR YOUR LIFE

God has placed a crown of His favor, peace, and permanent felicity upon my head.

teve bought his two-year-old daughter, Sarah, an aquarium. They went together to the pet store to pick out four fish to put into the tank. A few weeks later, Sarah found one of the fish dead, caught in one of the fake plastic bushes. Steve's wife called him at the office and said that Sarah had something to tell him. In her two-year-old vocabulary, she explained that the fish had died, she found it in the bushes, and she and Mommy were going to have a funeral for it in the backyard.

Steve realized that this was the first of many losses she would experience in life. But he broke into tears when the last thing she said before hanging up the phone was: "Daddy, keep me from getting caught in the bushes."

Your heavenly Father watches over you and keeps you from getting "caught in the bushes," trapped in circumstances or problems beyond your control. You are safe in His care!

He that dwelleth in the secret place of the most High shall abide under the shadow of the Almighty. I will say of the Lord, He is my refuge and my fortress: my God; in him will I trust.

PSALM 91:1–2 KJV

DECLARATION FOR YOUR LIFE

I dwell in the secret place of the Most High and rest, remaining steadfast and secure, under the shadow of the Almighty. He is my refuge and my fortress, my God and Father, and I trust Him with all of my heart.

hen does a nine-story fall not kill you? When you make a perfect landing.

What should have been a tragedy for Gloria Jummati turned out quite differently. While cleaning the balcony of her ninth-floor condominium, the seventy-year-old woman toppled over the railing. But Gloria never actually hit the ground. A small, forest-green door canopy broke her fall. Gloria landed in an ideal spot, right in the middle of the canvas-and-aluminum-pipe construction. A couple of inches in any direction, and the accident could have proven fatal. Instead, her landing was perfect. The pipes bent and cradled her body, stopping her just feet from the ground. She walked away with only a shoulder injury, thanking God for His angels of protection. Not even the canvas canopy was torn.

He shall give his angels charge over thee,
to keep thee in all thy ways. They shall
bear thee up in their hands, lest thou
dash thy foot against a stone.

PSALM 91:11–12 KJV

DECLARATION FOR YOUR LIFE

God has commanded the angels to set up camp around me as sentinels in my life. They guard me in all of my ways and keep me from all harm. They bear me up in their hands lest I dash my foot against a stone.

"HI, SPECIAL ONE!"

ill was kneeling in prayer in the front room of his house at 6:30 in the morning. He had just confessed his sins and was asking God for a blessing that day, needing to feel loved by Him.

His little boy, Timothy, who was just 22 months old, had just gotten up, and Bill noticed out of the corner of his eye that Timothy had sneaked quietly into the front room. He was always quiet in the morning when his dad was praying because his mom asked him to be, but that day, he ambled straight over to Bill, put a hand on his clasped hands, and said, "Hi, special one. Hi, special one. Hi, special one."

Never once had he called his dad that before. Six times he called Bill "special one." He said it enough for Bill to actually get it—that God was speaking to him and giving him a blessing, through his own little son.

Blessed is every one who fears the Lord,
Who walks in His ways.

PSALM 128:1 NKJV

DECLARATION FOR YOUR LIFE

I walk in the ways of almighty God as a good son/daughter and disciple. I eat the fruit of my labor and live my life in happiness, peace, divine favor, and good fortune of every kind.

man who was quite a lover of the hunt told the following story.

Rising early one morning, he said, "I heard the barking of a number of dogs chasing a deer. Looking at a large open field in front of me, I saw a young fawn making its way across the field and giving signs that its race was almost run. It leaped over the rails of the enclosed place and crouched within ten feet of where I stood. A moment later two of the hounds came over, and the fawn ran in my direction and pushed its head between my legs. I lifted the little thing to my breast, and, swinging round and round, fought off the dogs. Just then I felt that all the dogs in the West could not and would not capture that fawn after its weakness had appealed to my strength."

In the same way, the Lord protects His dear children from the threats of the enemy and holds them safe in His protective arms.

But the Lord is faithful, and he will strengthen and protect you from the evil one.

2 THESSALONIANS 3:3

DECLARATION FOR YOUR LIFE

The Lord is faithful. He strengthens me with His awesome power and protects me from the strategies of the evil one. My heavenly Father takes His stand as a sentinel in my life. He is ever alert and well able to maintain His covenant with me and bring me to victory in every situation.

Every Blessing Is Yours!

 our Father, the eternal God, is your Healer, your Refuge, and your Habitation. He has sent His Word and healed you from every disease! His everlasting arms hold you as a loving Father holds His child.

The Lord has driven the enemy from before you, and He has charged you with destroying the strongholds of the enemy in this earth.

Give thanks and praise to Him today that you live in safety and health under your Father's protection and care and live in the land of abundance that He has promised to you and to your children!

"For I will restore health to you
And heal you of your wounds," says the Lord,
   "Because they called you an outcast saying:
   'This is Zion;
No one seeks her.'"
Thus says the Lord:
   "Behold, I will bring back the captivity
      of Jacob's tents,
And have mercy on his dwelling places;
The city shall be built upon its own mound,
And the palace shall remain according to its
   own plan."

JEREMIAH 30:17–18 NKJV

DECLARATION FOR YOUR LIFE

God has restored health and vitality to me and has healed all of my wounds. He has compassion on my dwelling and restores to me all of the fortunes that the devil robbed from my life. Good health, prosperity, and God's tender care are ever-present realities for me to enjoy.

omeone asked Dwight Moody how he managed to remain so intimate in his relationship with Christ. He replied, *"I have come to Him as the best friend I have ever found, and I can trust Him in that relationship. I have believed He is Savior; I have believed He is God; I have believed He is my friend, and there isn't any problem in my life, there isn't any uncertainty in my work but I turn and speak to Him as naturally as to someone in the same room, and I have done it these years because I can trust Jesus."[7]*

I am not ashamed, for I know whom
I have believed and am persuaded
that He is able to keep what I have
committed to Him until that Day.

2 TIMOTHY 1:12 NKJV

DECLARATION FOR YOUR LIFE

*I know the One in whom I have believed, and I am
convinced that He is able to guard what I have entrusted
to Him. He is trustworthy—I can count on Him!*

mother gave her son a ticket to the football game. However, instead of enjoying the game, he spent the entire time walking around the ground collecting cans and bottles to pay her back for the price of the ticket.

"We didn't want him to work during the game," the mother said sadly. "We wanted him to enjoy it."

She said, "I'll never forget his sweaty little face as he told me he lacked only two bottles before he could pay us back. His father and I had thought all the time that he was enjoying the ball game with his friends."

Just as the boy did not have to do anything to earn the gift from his parents, so you do not have to do anything to earn the blessings of God in your life. All you must do is stand in faith and claim the promises. God's gifts are freely given!

Whatever you ask for in prayer, believe that you have received it, and it will be yours.

MARK 11:24

DECLARATION FOR YOUR LIFE

Everything that I believe with my heart and speak from my mouth, within the boundaries of God's Word, becomes reality for me. Whatever I ask for in prayer, if I believe I have received it, I will have it.

A Prayer of Gratitude

ord, I shudder to think about what my life would be like without You. I don't know where I'd be without Your loving hand guiding me. I need You so much! I am so thankful for Your presence in my life and Your great faithfulness to me. Your loving-kindness has changed my life. You are the stability and security of my life. You are the greatest treasure of my heart. So, I will trust You in the days ahead. I now receive Your strength and thank You for Your watchful care and protection over my life. I rejoice that I belong to You forever.

The Lord is my strength and my shield;
My heart trusted in Him, and I am helped;
Therefore my heart greatly rejoices,
And with my song I will praise Him.

PSALM 28:7 NKJV

DECLARATION FOR YOUR LIFE

The Lord is my ever-present helper. He is always there for me, and He brings me to victory no matter what situation or circumstance I find myself in. He is my strength and my shield, and I will trust in Him with a steadfast heart.

he story is told of a town where all the residents are ducks. Every Sunday the ducks waddle out of their houses and waddle down Main Street to their church. The duck minister comes forward and opens the duck Bible: "Ducks! God has given you wings! With wings you can fly! With wings you can mount up and soar like eagles!" All the ducks shout, "Amen!" *And then they all waddle back home.*

God's will is that you would receive *all* of the blessings that He has prepared for you. His great love has made provision for you to walk in these blessings, so don't waddle—learn how to fly above your circumstances and live the victorious life He has created you to live!

The young lions do lack, and suffer hunger:
but they that seek the Lord shall not want
any good thing.

PSALM 34:10 KJV

DECLARATION FOR YOUR LIFE

*Experience has proven that the Lord is good. I take my
refuge in Him and I am blessed. I have placed my
steadfast confidence in Him and I lack no good thing
in my life. Even the strongest in the world can become
weak and hungry, but I am sustained and given great
strength to persevere in every situation.*

His Bread—Your Sack

xplorer Ernest Shackleton headed an expedition to the South Pole. Near the end of their journey, food supplies were exhausted save for one last ration of hardtack, that was distributed to each man, some of whom saved it for later. After the weary men had gone to sleep, Shackleton said that out of the corner of his eye, he noticed one of his most trusted men looking about to see if anyone was watching.

Shackleton's heart sank within him as this man began to reach toward the sack of the man next to him. The man then opened the sack, took his own hardtack, and put it in the other man's sack.

The Lord wants to satisfy the deepest hungers that you have—body, soul, and spirit. He has taken His own "bread" and placed it into your "sack." Trust in Him and you will never hunger or thirst again.

Jesus said to them, "I am the bread of life. He who comes to Me shall never hunger, and he who believes in Me shall never thirst."

JOHN 6:35 NKJV

DECLARATION FOR YOUR LIFE

Jesus is the Bread of Life to me. I cling to Him with all of my heart. Because of Him, I will never hunger or thirst again.

Ask and You Shall Receive

olfer Arnold Palmer once played a series of exhibition matches in Saudi Arabia. The king was so impressed that he proposed to give Palmer a gift. Palmer demurred: "It really isn't necessary, Your Highness. I'm honored to have been invited."

"I would be deeply upset," replied the king, "if you would not allow me to give you a gift."

Palmer thought for a moment and said, "All right. How about a golf club? That would be a beautiful memento of my visit to your country."

The next day, delivered to Palmer's hotel, was the title to a golf club. Thousands of acres, trees, lakes, and a clubhouse.

There is a lesson to be learned from this story: In the presence of a king, don't ask for small gifts! The Lord, the King of the universe, longs to lavish His people with good gifts—we need only ask!

Ask, and it shall be given you; seek, and ye shall find; knock, and it shall be opened unto you: For every one that asketh receiveth; and he that seeketh findeth; and to him that knocketh it shall be opened.

MATTHEW 7:7–8 KJV

DECLARATION FOR YOUR LIFE

I know of a certainty that when I ask, I will receive; when I seek, I will find; and when I knock, the door will be opened to me.

forest fire had started near Bill's home, and although the firefighters had said it was under control, the Holy Spirit warned him that he and his family needed to evacuate.

The following morning was Sunday, and Bill's family asked their fellow church members for prayer. That day the fire burned very quickly, traveling down the canyon toward their home at speeds of up to fifty miles per hour. It came all the way up to their house, with temperatures nearing two thousand degrees. It blew out their propane tank and burned right up to within four feet of their house on all sides—but then it went around the house and continued burning, leaving the house unharmed.

The blessings of God rest on the righteous, protecting them and causing their ways to prosper.

He shall be like a tree
  Planted by the rivers of water,
  That brings forth its fruit in its season,
  Whose leaf also shall not wither;
And whatever he does shall prosper.

PSALM 1:3 NKJV

DECLARATION FOR YOUR LIFE

I am like a tree that is planted beside fresh-water springs. I bear the best of fruit in my life. Everything about me exudes life and everything that I set my hand to do prospers.

THE LIGHTHOUSE IN THE STORM

 urricane Isabel was front-page news in September 2003 as it rampaged through the Middle Atlantic states, coming ashore first in all its fury near Cape Hatteras, North Carolina, the site of one of America's most famous lighthouses.

When the storm hit Hatteras, the only road to the mainland was destroyed. Oceanfront houses were swept from their cement foundations and dropped elsewhere on the island. One entire hotel was deposited like a soggy cardboard box in the middle of a street. Appliances littered the ground. But the lighthouse on the tip of the island remained standing.

When you are a truly blessed child of God, no matter what storms may rage around your life, you will be able to remain firm and steadfast, strong, happy, and joyful in whatever circumstances life may bring.

In you, O Lord, I have taken refuge…
you are my rock and my fortress.

PSALM 71:1, 3

DECLARATION FOR YOUR LIFE

*My heavenly Father is a Rock where I can always go
and find refuge.*

GOD'S GREAT PLANS

hatever plans you have made for your life, God's plans for you are even better. He has chosen you and has only good things in store for you. You can rest assured and confident that He is not out to harm you, to "teach you a lesson" by bringing difficulties your way. No, His plans for you are good—entirely good— in every way!

Take the time to thank Him today for His goodness to you. Ask Him to reveal His good plans for your life. Look forward to your future with great hope, because God's great love for you will bring His good plans for you to pass.

"For I know the plans I have for you,"
declares the Lord, "plans to prosper you
and not to harm you, plans to give
you hope and a future."

JEREMIAH 29:11

DECLARATION FOR YOUR LIFE

All of God's thoughts for me are for good and never evil. His plan for my life is to make me prosperous, give me hope, and provide for me a glorious future. He has handpicked everything that is best for me in life and presents it to me with great joy. His desire for me is to live in His abundance.

Nigerian woman introduced herself to Megan using an American name. "What's your African name?" Megan asked. She immediately spoke it, several syllables long, with a musical sound.

"What does the name mean?" Megan wondered.

"It means 'Child who takes the anger away.'" The woman explained, "My parents had been forbidden by their parents to marry. But they loved each other so much that they defied the family opinions and married anyway. For several years they were ostracized, but then they became pregnant with me. When the grandparents held me in their arms, the walls of hostility came down, and that's why my parents gave me that name."

Jesus is the Child who has taken down the walls of hostility between you and your heavenly Father. He has established peace in your life and showers you with an abundance of blessings!

Lord, you establish peace for us;
   all that we have accomplished you have
      done for us.

ISAIAH 26:12

DECLARATION FOR YOUR LIFE

My heavenly Father has ordained peace, favor, and an abundance of blessings for me. He has worked in and through me to achieve all that I have done. What a privilege it is to be in such an incredible partnership!

NOTES

1. Leslie B. Flynn, *19 Gifts of the Spirit* (Wheaton, IL: Victor, 1975), 203–204.

2. Elisabeth Elliot, *Shadow of the Almighty* (Grand Rapids, Mich.: Zondervan, 1958), 85.

3. Vance Havner, *Hearts Afire* (Old Tappan, NJ: Fleming Revell Co., 1952).

4. Randy Bishop, "Just Give Me Jesus" *Christian Reader* Sept./Oct. 2000, 25.

5. Norman P. Grubb, C. T. Studd, *Cricketer and Pioneer* (London: Religious Tract Society, 1933), 52–53.

6. Flynn.

7. William M. Anderson, *The Faith That Satisfies* (New York: Loizeaux Brothers, 1948), 165.

Celebrate God's grace in your life beginning today.

In a world that is oftentimes unkind and unloving, the good news is that a loving God has chosen you to be His own.

God knows you far better than you know yourself and has designed a specific destiny for you—something only you personally can fulfill. Even if you feel that you have missed your opportunity, know that God is not moved by time as we are. His purpose for your life is waiting. Embrace the love that God has for you. Be assured that when God calls you by name, He is also patient and persistent and is always ready when you are.

Chosen by God will help your spirit soar through daily reminders of just how much you matter to God.

Chosen by God • 1-57794-803-3
Available at bookstores everywhere
or visit **www.harrisonhouse.com**.

www.harrisonhouse.com

Fast. Easy. Convenient!

- ◆ New Book Information
- ◆ Look Inside the Book
- ◆ Press Releases
- ◆ Bestsellers
- ◆ Free E-News
- ◆ Author Biographies

- ◆ Upcoming Books
- ◆ Share Your Testimony
- ◆ Online Product Availability
- ◆ Product Specials
- ◆ Order Online

For the latest in book news and author information, please visit us on the Web at www.harrisonhouse.com. Get up-to-date pictures and details on all our powerful and life-changing products. Sign up for our e-mail newsletter, *Friends of the House*, and receive free monthly information on our authors and products including testimonials, author announcements, and more!

Harrison House—
Books That Bring Hope, Books That Bring Change

THE HARRISON HOUSE VISION

Proclaiming the truth and the power
Of the Gospel of Jesus Christ
With excellence;

Challenging Christians to
Live victoriously,
Grow spiritually,
Know God intimately.